for Jim and Vi

SIGHT SINGING MADE SIMPLE

An Audio Course for Group or Self Study

By David Bauguess

HAL•LEONARD® CORPORATION
7777 W. BLUEMOUND RD. P.O. BOX 13819 MILWAUKEE, WI 53213

INTRODUCTION

To The Student

Sight Singing Made Simple is a unique program that goes beyond merely teaching *about* the symbols of music. It let's you *hear* the sounds the symbols represent, and it introduces you to a method of reading music and gives you an opportunity to practice your new skill. This course assumes you know nothing about reading music. We're going to start at the very beginning. Our goal is to understand the symbols of written music, and more importantly, get you started actually reading music.

Sight Singing Made Simple consists of two components: an audio recording and this accompanying book. As you progress through the course you will be introduced to various concepts about how music is represented graphically on the printed page — called *notation* — and how sound is organized in musical ways — called *music theory*. As terms and symbols are introduced on the recording, you will be referred to examples in the book. The back of this book contains a Glossary of these terms and symbols for convenient reference. The book also contains many exercises for practice.

The ability to read music is a skill that relatively few people possess, and yet it is an invaluable key to the joy of learning music through performance. *Sight Singing Made Simple* is your key to learning the fundamentals of music reading quickly and enjoyably.

To The Teacher

Sight Singing Made Simple is a course in the fundamentals of reading music. It has been designed to be used by individuals; and although a teacher would be a helpful resource, one is not required.

Sight Singing Made Simple will be an effective tool in a variety of situations, including self-study, private music lessons, and for singers in school, college, church and community choirs. A teacher may also use it to introduce music reading to a choir or a class. (Additional books may be purchased separately for group use.)

The inspiration for the development of *Sight Singing Made Simple* was to address a common problem experienced by choral directors: *What do I do when non-readers join a choir that can read music? How can I catch up non-readers so they can participate in sight singing practice? Sight Singing Made Simple* was designed to answer this need with ease and efficiency.

In a choral setting, the recording and book can be used by a singer for individual study during rehearsal and/or at home. Since *Sight Singing Made Simple* is a compact introduction to the basics, it cannot accomplish in a few hours what a choir has accomplished over the course of many weeks; but it can introduce the workings of notation and a method of reading music so that the singer can benefit from the choir's on-going sight reading training. Needless to say, any monitoring of progress you can provide will benefit the student.

Sight Singing Made Simple teaches movable Do solfège. Teachers should, therefore, find it helpful as an introduction to any published sight singing method using movable Do. For the comfort of the voice, all exercises are pitched in a one octave range from B♭ to B♭. Rhythms covered include whole, half, dotted half, quarter, eighth notes, rests, ties, and simple meters with a quarter note beat. Melodic exercises include stepwise movement and tonic chord skips.

The book is set up so that a group or individual can work on only as much as they need or can handle. Refer to the **Summary of Material** chart on page 5 to see an overview of the course's sequence. For best results, make sure the students have fully grasped the concepts in one section before moving on.

HOW TO USE THIS AUDIO COURSE

Read this page before starting the recording

To begin, simply start the recording and follow along in this book beginning on page 6. Be prepared to stop or pause your player when you need to or are instructed to. **If the CD is being used, make sure you press pause instead of stop to avoid returning to Track #1 each time.** Look for these symbols for starting and stopping or pausing your player:

START **Start Recording**

STOP **Stop or Pause Recording**

The narration you will hear on the recording is in shaded boxes throughout this book. The examples, exercises and self-study items will appear following their introduction on the recording. Especially important are key words that are printed in bold and defined after they are introduced in the narration. They are also included in the Glossary at the end of the book.

Whenever you see this symbol,

MUSIC LISTENING **Music Listening Example**

it means that you will hear an example of music on the recording which is not printed in the book. This is your cue to listen and concentrate on what you hear, as this is one of the most important aspects of learning to read music.

Tips For Getting The Most From This Course

- Use good quality playback equipment for the recording. Look for good speaker sound. Headphones will work for listening only—not for practicing reading.
- If your playback equipment has a balance control, you will be able to select the channel for either the male or female voice, if you want.
- If you are using a cassette player, select these options if they are available to you: turn on Dolby (Dolby B), and use Normal (Type I) Bias and Equalization.
- If your cassette player has a counter, set it at zero at the beginning of the tape, and keep a pencil and paper handy to jot down the counter number for the beginning of the major section breaks (listed in the Summary of Material). Track numbers in this book refer to track numbers for the Compact Disc.
- Select a quiet environment where you can concentrate and will not be disturbed by other activity or music.
- Try to work in short, focused sessions. Take a break when your concentration fades.
- Work with each section of the material as much as you need to until you have a good grasp of it. Refer to the Summary of Material on page 5 for a breakdown of the sections.
- Use the Glossary of Terms on pages 37-41.
- If possible, have someone who reads music check your progress.
- Don't take yourself too seriously. Have fun!

SUMMARY OF MATERIAL

CONTENTS

*Because of the variances in cassette players, you will need to fill in the cassette count from your player throughout the book. Make sure your player is set on 000 before you begin.

SIDE 1

Track #1 START Cassette Count*000

Welcome to *Sight Singing Made Simple*. We're confident you'll find this program to be an effective method for learning the basics of how to read music. *Sight Singing Made Simple* can be your key to a whole new level of participation and enjoyment in music.

Reading music is easier than you might expect. The basics can be learned in a relatively short period of time, with a modest amount of practice. As with most any skill, continued practice is necessary if you want to be good at it.

Basically, music reading consists of only two things:

1. knowing how high or low to make a sound, and
2. knowing how long to hold the sound

The term we use to refer to the highness or lowness of musical sounds is **pitch**. The time element in music is called **rhythm**, and how long sounds are held is **duration**.

Since music is an art form that takes place in time, we must have a way of measuring the time we hold pitches. Visually, we have units of measure such as inches and feet, meters and millimeters. We measure time in units of hours, minutes and seconds. In music, the unit for measuring time is the **beat**. The beat is the pulse of music — that aspect we often respond to by clapping, snapping our fingers, or tapping our feet.

MUSIC LISTENING

Notice the steady evenness of the beat, like the ticking of a clock.

In reading music, we use the beat as a measure of how long we'll hold each pitch. Some pitches will last one beat, some two beats or longer, others only a portion of a beat.

Notation is a set of visual symbols used to represent musical sounds. It's what we often see on the printed page and call "music." But, in fact, music is sound. What we see in print is notation — graphic symbols representing musical sounds. Reading music is the process of making the sounds those symbols represent.

The symbols we use to represent the time or duration of sound are called **notes**. The symbol we'll use to represent one beat of time is the quarter note.

Study the information below before listening to the next musical exercises. When you're familiar with each of the symbols and terms, start the recording again.

STOP

Symbol:	♩	𝅗𝅥	𝅗𝅥.	𝅝
Note Name:	quarter note	half note	dotted half note	whole note
Beat Value:	1 beat	2 beats	3 beats	4 beats

Ta is used to sound out the rhythms. It has no special meaning, but simply works well because the T makes it clear where each note starts, and the ah is a comfortable vowel on which to sustain the note for its proper duration.

Voice: Ta Ta Ta Ta Ta__ Ta__ Ta____ Ta______

Notes: ♩ ♩ ♩ ♩ 𝅗𝅥 𝅗𝅥 𝅗𝅥. 𝅝

The Beat: • • • • • • • • • • • • • • • • • (*Heard as clicks on the recording.*)

The final click in each exercise represents the point at which the last beat *ends*. It is not an extra beat.

Key Words:

pitch – highness or lowness of musical sound
rhythm – the time element in music
duration – how long sounds are held
beat – the "pulse" of music and the unit used to measure the duration of sounds
notation – musical symbols used to visually represent musical sound
notes – the symbols we use to represent the time or duration of sound

Track #2 START Cassette Count____

Here are examples of the four notes. The clicks represent the beat. The notes are voiced on Ta.

Here's what four quarter notes sound like:

TaTaTaTa
• • • •

The half note is held the duration of two beats:

Ta__Ta__Ta__Ta__
• • • • • • • • •

Here's the dotted half note, held for three beats:

Ta___Ta___Ta___
• • • • • • • • • •

And the whole note, held for four beats:

Ta____Ta____
• • • • • • • • •

The best way to learn to read music is to actually read it, so let's start by practicing sounding the duration of notes. You'll hear four beats before each exercise begins. We'll sound each note with a "Ta." Point to each note as you sound it out.

EXERCISE 1

Remember to point to each note as you sound it. Here's Exercise 2.

EXERCISE 2

As a learning aid you may find it helpful in practicing to give a little pulse or emphasis to the second beat of half notes, Ta-a Ta-a. The same can be done with the second and third beats of dotted half notes, Ta-a-a, and beats 2, 3, and 4 of whole notes, Ta-a-a-a. Let's try it on Exercise 3.

EXERCISE 3

Let's make a couple of observations about the beat. First, it's steady and even. Second, the speed of the beat can be different for each exercise or song. Here's a song sung with rather long beats:

MUSIC LISTENING

The shorter the duration of the beat, the "faster" a piece of music sounds to us. Here's the same song with a shorter beat:

MUSIC LISTENING

The speed of music is referred to as the **tempo**. So, we might describe a song as having a slow tempo, a moderate tempo, or a fast tempo.

Exercise 4 is a special exercise. You are given a large box divided into four columns and four rows, resulting in sixteen smaller boxes. Each box contains various combinations of notes, each adding up to four beats of time. By the way, it makes no difference whether the long "stem" of the note goes up or down. You see it both ways in this exercise.

Study the instructions and then practice Exercise 4.

STOP

Key Word:
tempo – the speed of the music, determined by the length of the beat

INSTRUCTIONS FOR EXERCISE 4:

1. Set a slow or moderate tempo by tapping a foot or finger or clapping lightly. Continue tapping or clapping the beat as you voice the exercise.
2. Sound the notes in each box, moving from left to right across the first row and then down to the next row and across—just like you read a book. Sound each note on Ta.
3. Move with a steady beat and no pause in going from one box to the next.

NOTE: Exercise 4 is not on the recording. This is for your individual practice.

For additional benefit from Exercise 4, practice at a faster tempo. Also try reading in a different order:

- down the first column, then down the second column, etc.
- backwards
- randomly hop around from box to box

It's like writing your own exercises!

EXERCISE 4

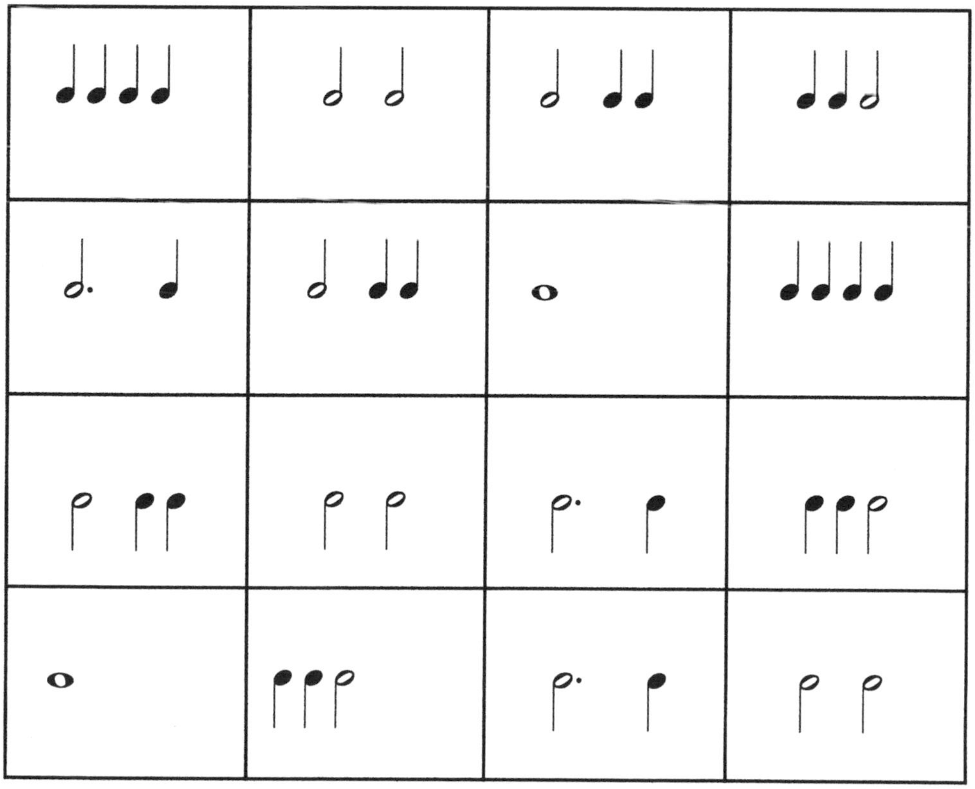

Track #3 START Cassette Count____

Music is not always continuous sound. Momentary silence in a vocal or instrumental part is common. For example, in a choir, the basses may sing for about a minute, stop for a few seconds, and then resume singing. When they stop, and their part is momentarily silent, we say they are "resting." While they rest, it's necessary for them to keep track of time so they know exactly when to start singing again. To do this we use a set of symbols called rests that represent silence. As with notes, the duration of rests is measured by the beat.

As you see below, rests are named after notes; and each rest has the same beat value as its corresponding note. For example, the quarter note and the quarter rest both have a duration of one beat. Before going on, take a moment to memorize the values of the rests shown below.

STOP

Key Word:

rests – the symbols of musical notation that represent silence.

Symbol:			
Note Name:	quarter rest	half rest	whole rest
Beat Value:	1 beat	2 beats	4 beats

Pay special attention to the difference between the half rest, which *sits* on a line, and the whole rest, which *hangs* from a line. For three beats of rest, the combination of a half rest and a quarter rest is used rather than a dotted half rest.

Track #4 START Cassette Count____

Exercise 5 incorporates rests. Voice each note on Ta and be silent for the duration of each rest. Remember to point to each note and rest as you go through the exercise.

EXERCISE 5

The next two exercises also mix rests with notes. As you practice, give careful attention to holding each note for its full beat length.

EXERCISE 6

EXERCISE 7

You'll recognize Exercise 8 as being similar to Exercise 4. The instructions in your book for Exercise 4 (on page 9) also apply to Exercise 8. Stop the recording now and practice Exercise 8.

EXERCISE 8

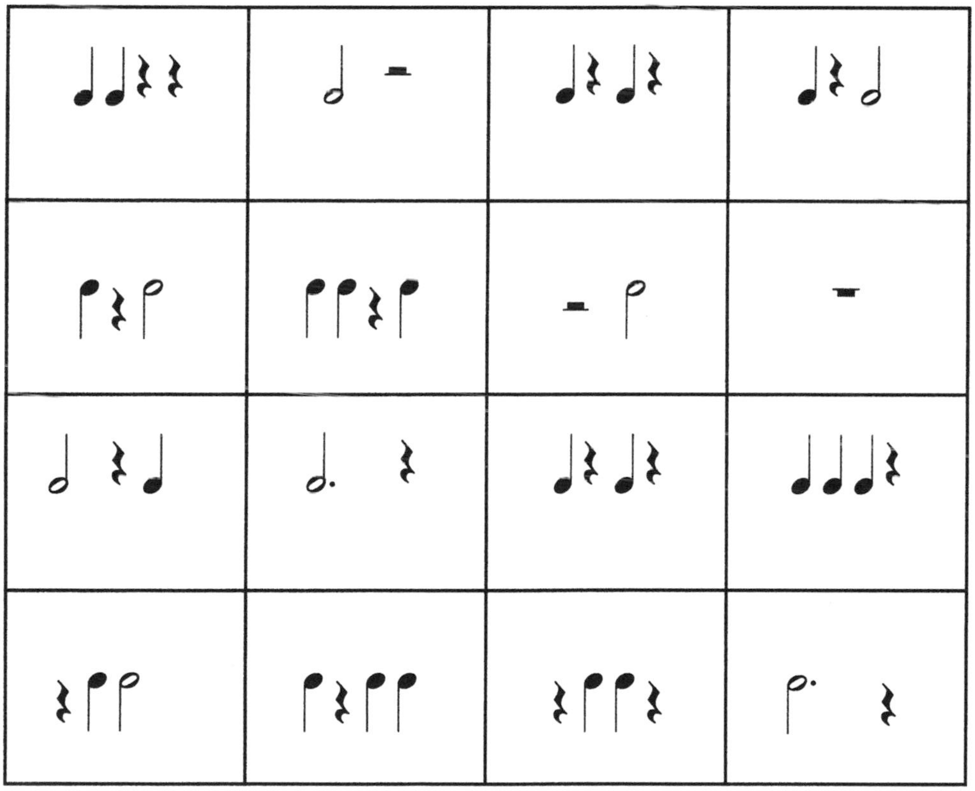

Track #5 START Cassette Count____

I'm sure you're aware that some beats in music are given greater emphasis than others. Instead of the beat sounding like this: ta ta ta ta ta ta ta ta, it sounds more like this: **Ta** ta ta **Ta** ta ta **Ta** ta ta (or) **Ta** ta ta ta **Ta** ta ta ta.

The musical term for stressing a beat in this manner is **accent**. When beats are accented in a regular pattern, it has the effect of grouping the beats. A common grouping is four beats per group: **1** 2 3 4 **1** 2 3 4 **Ta** ta ta ta **Ta** ta ta ta. The grouping is accomplished by accenting.

MUSIC LISTENING

Another common grouping is three beats per group: **1** 2 3 **1** 2 3 **Ta** ta ta **Ta** ta ta. Each accented beat 1 starts a new group.

In music, the grouping of beats by accents is called **meter**. Each group is called a **measure** or a **bar**.

We need to be aware of meter in music because accenting is an important part of the sound of music and is therefore important in reading music; also, several symbols of musical notation pertain to meter.

One way accenting is indicated in notation is by placing an accent symbol > by the note to be accented. It looks like the "greater than" sign used in math. Let's read Exercise 9 on Ta. Be sure to make the accented notes "greater than" the unaccented notes!

Key Words:

accent – > stress or emphasize notes by singing or playing them louder.
meter – the grouping of beats by accents.
measure – a group of beats, the first of which is accented. Also called a **bar**.

EXERCISE 9

Meter is indicated in music by a symbol called the **meter signature** (also called the **time signature**). The meter signature is a pair of numbers, arranged like a fraction, that appears at the beginning of a piece of music.

The information below shows three common meter signatures: $\frac{2}{4}$ $\frac{3}{4}$ and $\frac{4}{4}$

The top number of the meter signature tells how many beats of time are in each measure. The bottom number indicates what kind of note is used to represent one beat. Study the information below.

STOP

Key Word:

meter signature – a sign consisting of two numbers which indicates meter. The top number is the number of beats (or total beats worth of time) per measure. The bottom number represents the note that equals one beat. Also called the **time signature**.

Indicates the number of beats of time per measure →	2	3	4
Indicates the kind of note that represents one beat →	4	4	4 ← ♩ = $\frac{1}{(4)}$ note

Track #6 START Cassette Count____

In notation, measures are set apart with **bar lines**. Instead of writing an accent on each first beat, it is understood in reading music that when you cross over the bar line, you accent the note on the first beat. Of course, if there's a rest on the first beat, there is nothing to accent. Exercise 10 is the same as Exercise 9, except it is notated with a meter signature and bar lines. Notice also that a **double bar** is used to indicate the end of the music.

STOP

Key Words:

bar lines – vertical lines placed on the staff to indicate the end of one measure and the beginning of another.
double bar – vertical lines (one thin and one thick) placed on the staff to indicate the end of music.

Compare the notation of Exercises 9 and 10.

Track #7 START Cassette Count____

Let's sound out Exercise 10. Remember to accent the first beat when you cross over the bar line.

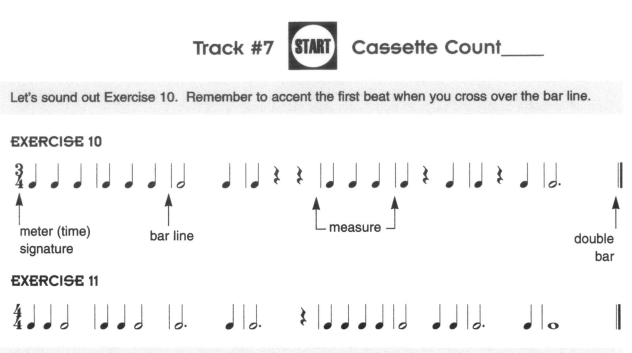

EXERCISE 10

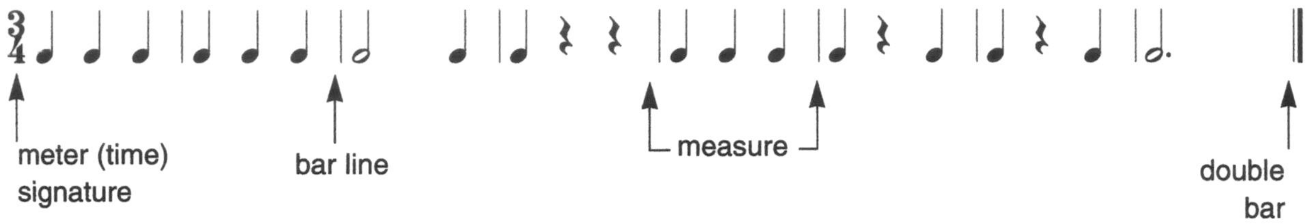

EXERCISE 11

The value of two notes can be "added" together into what sounds like one note. The symbol for this is the **tie**. For example, a tied half note and quarter note is equal to three beats and is sounded as if it were a dotted half note. See below for some illustrations of how the tie works.

STOP

Key Word:

tie – A curved line connecting two successive notes which are on the same line or space and are of identical pitch. Tied notes sound as if they were a single note of the combined value of the notes that are tied.

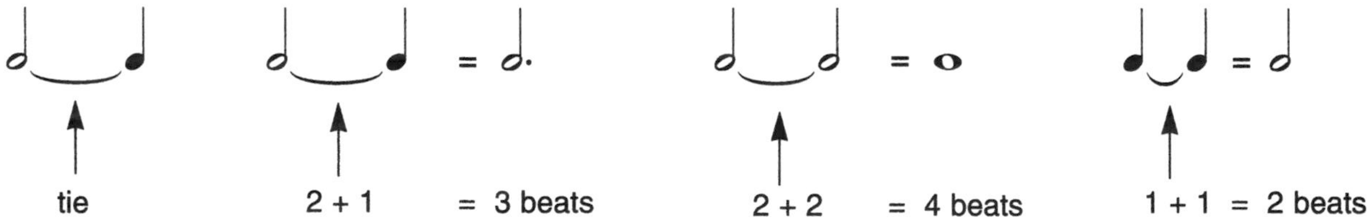

Track #8 START Cassette Count____

EXERCISE 12

EXERCISE 13

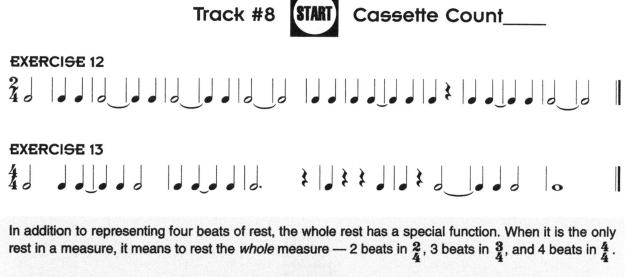

In addition to representing four beats of rest, the whole rest has a special function. When it is the only rest in a measure, it means to rest the *whole* measure — 2 beats in $\frac{2}{4}$, 3 beats in $\frac{3}{4}$, and 4 beats in $\frac{4}{4}$.

In other words, rest the number of beats in that measure.

EXERCISE 14

EXERCISE 15

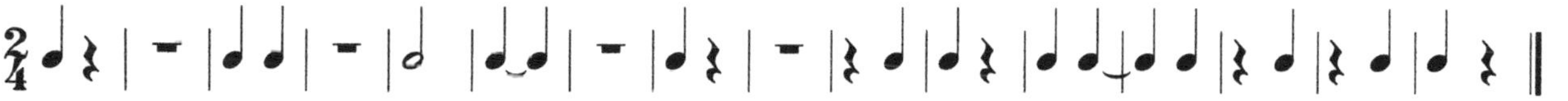

EXERCISE 16

At this point we're ready to move on to reading pitch; but before we do, I encourage you to review Exercises 10-16. Also, try reading them without the recording and at faster tempos.

STOP

Track #9 START Cassette Count____

Listen to this song:

MUSIC LISTENING

Pitch is the highness and lowness of musical sounds. Like much of the music we hear, this song is constructed with seven different pitches. This arrangement of pitches and rhythm is the **melody** of the song we know as *America* or *God Save The Queen.* If I were to line up the seven different pitches of this melody from low to high it would sound like this:

MUSIC LISTENING

Doing this is very much like taking a short story and making an alphabetical list of the words used to write the story. We could call it a vocabulary list. In music the "listing" of pitches used to write a song is called a **scale**. Usually, in playing or singing a scale, we add a higher "version" of the first pitch at the top, so it sounds like this:

MUSIC LISTENING

When you hear the word "cat," it immediately triggers an image of a cat in your mind. This is because you have *associated* the sound of the word "cat" with what a cat looks like. We also make very strong associations with a person's name and their personal characteristics, such as appearance and personality.

Just as each word has its own meaning, so, in music each of the seven pitches of the scale has a unique quality of sound that distinguishes it. It is therefore, possible for us to give a name to each pitch, and, with practice, build a strong association with the name of the pitch and what it sounds like.

Reading pitch, then, consists of three simple steps:

1. Identify a note by its name.
2. Know what the pitch of that name sounds like.
3. Sing the pitch.

This method of reading music is called **solfège**.

The choice of names for the notes depends on the teacher. Some use **numbers** — 1 for the first pitch of the scale, 2 for the second and so forth. Others prefer syllable names: Do re mi fa so la ti. We'll be using **syllables** in the exercises on this recording.

Our goal is to learn to read music at "first sight" — without prior preparation. When we do this, we can say that we are **sight reading**, or **sight singing**, since we are using our voices. **Solfège** is a method of sight singing that uses syllables to name the pitches.

STOP

Key Words:

pitch – the highness or lowness of musical sounds

melody – the arrangement of pitches and rhythm

scale – a set of pitches used to compose a piece of music.

sight reading – the ability to read (sing or play) music at "first sight," i.e. without prior preparation.
sight singing – refers specifically to vocal sight reading.

syllables – single syllable names given to the tones of a scale for use in sight singing training and practice. Syllables are notably used in solfège.

solfège – the study of sight singing through the use of syllables.

Track #10 START **Cassette Count____**

Our first stop in reading pitch will be to get familiar with the sound of some of the patterns of pitches that we'll be working with. We're going to do this with a set of drills we'll call "Echo Drills." Instructions for how to do the Echo Drills are given in the book as Exercise 17.

STOP

EXERCISE 17
Echo Drills

The Echo Drills consist of two sets of four drills, each drill consisting of several short pitch patterns. Your job is to "echo" back each pattern just as you heard it. We'll go through these drills three times in three different ways.

NOTE: These drills are not in this book, so there's nothing you need to watch. In fact, you'll probably find your concentration sharpened by closing your eyes as you do them.

1. The first time through, echo each pattern in your mind as clearly as you can. Don't sing out loud; just try to "hear" the pattern repeated *in your mind* right after you hear it sung on the recording. Start the recording to hear a demonstration.

Track #11 START **Cassette Count____**

This recording track of the echo drills is for both the first and second times you go through them. Here is a brief demonstration of the Exercise with a voice echoing each pattern as in the second time through the drills.

MUSIC LISTENING

STOP (Select Track #11 or rewind cassette for the second time through.)

2. The second time is just like the first, but this time you will sing each pattern out loud. Imitate the singers as closely as you can. Back up the recording to repeat the track you played for the first time through.

Track #11 START **Cassette Count____**

This recording track of the echo drills is for both the first and second times you go through them. Here is a brief demonstration of the exercise with a voice echoing each pattern as in the second time through the drills.

MUSIC LISTENING

STOP

3. The third time through, each pattern will be sung with the syllable name for each pitch. Imitate what you hear by singing it out loud. Continue the recording where you left off.

Track #12 START **Cassette Count____**

This recording track of the echo drills is for the third time using the solfège syllables. Here's a demonstration:

MUSIC LISTENING

If needed, continue practicing the Echo Drills, until you find them very easy.

STOP

Track #13 START **Cassette Count____**

Another helpful preparation for the upcoming exercises is to practice singing the scale with syllable names. See Exercise 18 in your book, and let's sing it together.

EXERCISE 18

The Scale

Do re mi fa so la ti Do 𝄽 Do ti la so fa mi re Do

In singing the scale, you moved from one pitch to the next without skipping over any pitches. This is movement by step. Now, if I sing Do to Mi, it is not a step because I skip over Re. Therefore, I have moved by skip. See examples in the book.

Practice singing the scale until it is easy to sing quickly and from memory.

STOP

Key Words:

step – When we move from a pitch to the pitch that is immediately above or below it in the scale, we say that we have moved by step. Here are some examples of movement by step:

Do *to* Re   So *to* La   Fa *to* Mi   Ti *to* Do   Mi *to* Re

skip – In singing the scale you moved by step from one pitch to the next. If, in moving from one pitch to another, one or more pitches are skipped over, the movement is said to be by skip. Some examples of movement by skip are:

Do *to* Mi   So *to* Do   Re *to* So   Do *to* Fa   Mi *to* So

NOTE: For the remainder of the course, the recording will mostly consist of exercises. Most explanations of new concepts will be presented in the book. Key Words are still in bold and are explained in the text and/or in the Glossary of Terms on pages 37-41. So, it is especially important that you pause or stop the recording and take a moment to study new material when it is introduced.

Track #14 START **Cassette Count____**

We're going to continue our practice now with a series of exercises that move by step. (We'll take up skips later.) Since these exercises combine rhythm *and* pitch, resulting in a **melody**, they can be described as *melodic* exercises. In these first melodic exercises, pitch is indicated in your music by the first letter of each syllable name: D for Do, R for Re, and so forth. Each pitch is one beat long.

Your book describes the introduction we'll use with each exercise; listen to a demonstration with Exercise 19.

MUSIC LISTENING

Introduction to Exercises

Beginning with Exercise 19, each of the pitched exercises will be preceded with a short introduction. Here's what you'll hear:

- The pitch for Do is played
- Do-mi-so-mi-do is sung
- The first pitch of the exercise is sung
- Two beats sound
- The exercise begins

Let's do Exercise 19 together.

In Exercises 19-28 each syllable letter is one beat long.

EXERCISE 19

D r m r | D r m f | s f m r | D D r 𝄽 | D r m f | m f s f | m r D r | D t D 𝄽 ||

EXERCISE 20

D r m m | f m r 𝄽 | D r m f | s s s 𝄽 | s f s f | m r m 𝄽 | m f m r | D r D 𝄽 ||

EXERCISE 21

D t D r | m r m f | s f m r | r m r 𝄽 | D t D r | D r m f | m f s f | m r D 𝄽 ||

EXERCISE 22

s f m m | f m r r | D r m r | m f s 𝄽 | s f m m | f m r r | D r m r | r D D 𝄽 ||

STOP

Getting The Most Benefit From The Melodic Exercises

In addition to singing along with the voices on the recording, you can gain an even greater benefit from the melodic (pitched) exercises by also practicing in the following ways:

1. Sing along with the recording "mentally." In other words, instead of singing out loud, try to "hear" each sound in your mind just before the voices on the recording sing it. This will develop your "inner, musical ear."

2. When you feel ready, stop the recording right after the introduction, and sing the exercise by yourself. This will strengthen your independence.

3. As in number 2, sing the exercise without the recording, but do it at a faster tempo. This will improve the quickness of your mind.

Track #15 START Cassette Count____

EXERCISE 23

m f s f | m f s s | f m r D | r m r 𝄽 | D r m f | s f m r | m f s f | m r m 𝄽 ||

EXERCISE 24

D t l s | l t D r | D t D t | l s s 𝄽 | s l t D | r D t l | s l t t | D t D 𝄽 ||

EXERCISE 25

D t l l | s l t t | D r m r | D t t 𝄽 | D t l l | s s l s | l t l t | D r D 𝄽 ||

EXERCISE 26

s s l l | t l s s | l t D r | D D t 𝄽 | D t t l | s l s s | l t l t | t D D 𝄽 ||

EXERCISE 27

m r D r | m r D D | t l l s | l s s 𝄽 | l t D t | D r m m | r D D t | t 𝄽 D 𝄽 ||

EXERCISE 28

D 𝄽 r 𝄽 | m 𝄽 r 𝄽 | D r m f | s 𝄽 𝄽 s | s 𝄽 f 𝄽 | m 𝄽 m 𝄽 | r D r m | m r 𝄽 D ||

We're now going to take a big step forward in learning to read music—we're going to read pitch from notation.

Since pitch has to do with the highness and lowness of sounds, it is helpful to see this represented visually in notation. This is done with a musical symbol called the **staff**. The staff consists of five parallel lines on which notes are placed on the lines and on the spaces between the lines. See below.

The five horizontal, parallel lines on which notes are placed to show pitch is known as the **staff**.

The Staff

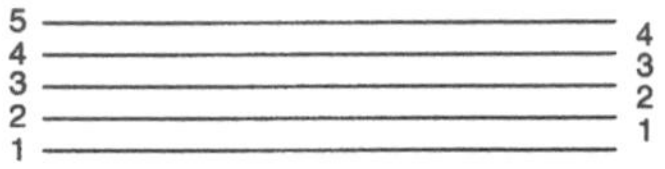

Numbers are referring to specific lines and spaces

The following illustration shows a scale written on the staff in two ways. One with letters representing the syllable names, and the other with notes. The letters and notes are placed on the lines and spaces of the staff. Notice that the scale's movement by step shows up on the staff as movement from line to space, and space to line.

The Scale

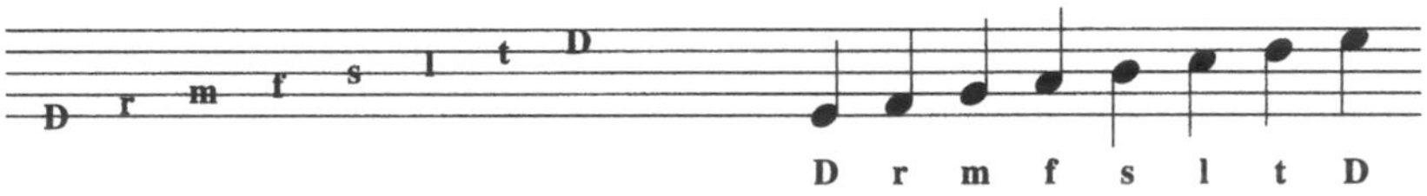

On the staff, movement by step is from a line to the space right above it or below it. Or, if a note is on a space, a step away is to the line right above it or below it.

The following illustration shows how notes on the staff are named. Take a moment to study this in the four melodies below.

Naming Notes On The Staff

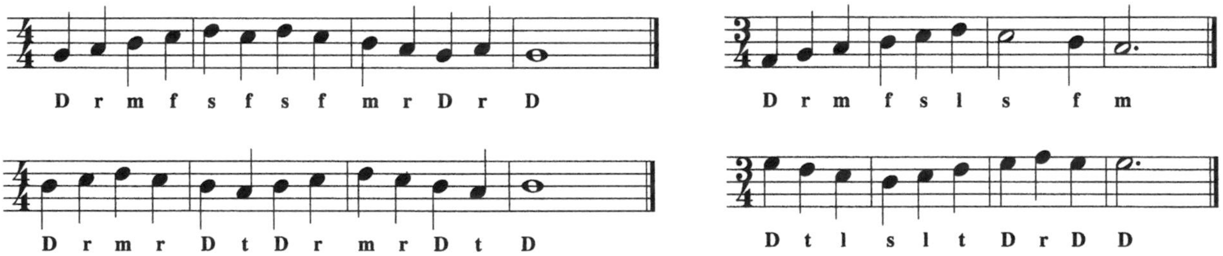

A comparison of the four melodies reveals a very important point: *Do can be located anywhere on the staff; all the other scale pitches are located in relation to where Do is.* If Do is on a line, Re is always on the space right above it; Mi is two steps above on the next line. If Do is on a space, Re is on the line above it, and Mi is on the next space, etc.

This system of solfège — in which Do can be any pitch, located anywhere on the staff — is called **movable Do solfège**.

Track #16 START SIDE 2 Cassette Count____

In our next exercises, you'll be given the syllable name of the starting note. All of the other notes, you will name as you sing them! Although we haven't worked together for very long, and I don't know you well, I just have a feeling you might be tempted to write in the names of those notes! Perish the thought! For the sake of developing your skill, be willing to struggle a little in the learning process! Practice the exercises as much as you want. It does get easier!

EXERCISE 29

EXERCISE 30

The letter C in the place of the meter signature is the symbol for **Common Time** which is the same as the $\frac{4}{4}$ meter signature.

EXERCISE 31

The symbol above the last note is a **fermata**. A note with a fermata is to be held somewhat longer than its normal value.

EXERCISE 32

EXERCISE 33

At the end of Exercise 34, the double bar with the double dots is a **repeat sign**. When you arrive at the sign, go back to the beginning and repeat the entire exercise.

EXERCISE 34

EXERCISE 35

The lines and spaces of the staff can hold nine different pitches. Two additional notes can be written on the staff by using the "space" just below the first line and just above the fifth line. However, eleven places for notes is not enough. The staff often needs to be extended to hold additional notes. This is accomplished with a musical symbol called the **ledger line**. See below to see how the ledger lines work.

STOP

Ledger lines are short horizontal lines that can be placed above and below the staff, in such a manner as to add both lines and spaces to the staff. A note can be placed on the ledger line or on the space above or below it. In reading and naming notes, remember that stepwise movement is always from line to space and from space to line—including the lines and spaces created by ledger lines. Observe how the notes in these examples are named.

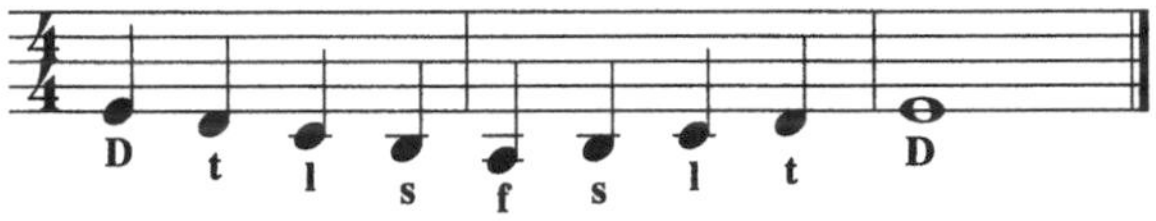

Track #17 START **Cassette Count____**

EXERCISE 36

EXERCISE 37

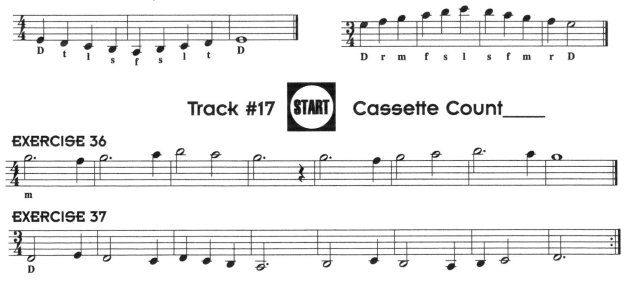

Your reading now, involves the two elements of pitch and rhythm. If you find that both are challenging you at the same time, you'll probably find it helpful to "divide and conquer." Practice the rhythm separately, then combine it with pitch.

It's helpful in reading rhythms to have a method. One of the most widely-used methods involves counting the beats of the measure. This method is explained below so read about it before we do the next exercises.

STOP

Reading Rhythms

The method for counting rhythms as an aid to reading works like this:

- Check the meter signature to see how many beats there are per measure.
- Each quarter note will be counted with the number of the beat it is in the measure. If a quarter note is the third beat in the measure, call it 3. If a quarter note is the second beat in the measure, call it 2.

- If the note is longer than a quarter note (and that includes tied notes) count it with the number of the beat it starts on and hold it out with just that number. A half note that begins on beat 3 and lasts through beat 4 will be called 3.

- Count rests silently to yourself.

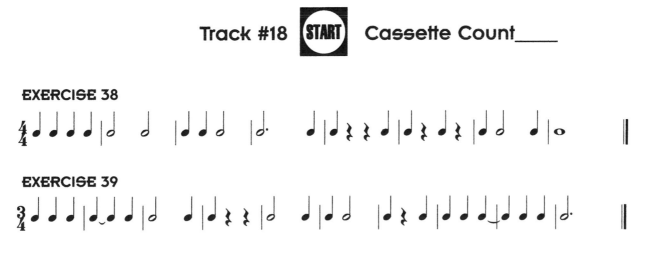

- Maintain a steady beat and point to each note as you count.

Use this method to count Exercises 38 and 39. Study them before you start the recording.

Track #18 START **Cassette Count____**

EXERCISE 38

EXERCISE 39

STOP

Before starting the recording for Exercises 40 through 42, try counting the rhythm of these exercises. Remember to keep a steady beat and point as you count.

Track #19 START Cassette Count____

EXERCISE 40

Exercise 41 begins with an incomplete measure — incomplete in that it does not contain the full number of beats indicated by the meter signature. Actually, the measure is split up and the remainder of it is at the end — one beat at the beginning and two at the end, which adds up to a complete measure of three beats. The single beat at the beginning is called a **pick-up** or **upbeat**. It is the last beat of the measure — beat 3. Beats 1 and 2 are in the last measure. Remember to accent beat 1 when you cross the bar line following the pick-up.

EXERCISE 41

Exercise 42 begins with three pick-up beats—beats 2, 3 & 4. Beat 1, that completes the measure, is at the end. As you already know, the first beat of a measure is accented. When the meter is four beats per measure, there is also a light accent on beat 3. In Exercise 42, accent the second of the three pick-up beats. The second note is beat 3. An accent has been written above the note to remind you.

EXERCISE 42

This would be a good point to review before going on.

STOP

Track #20 START Cassette Count____

We're now going to practice exercises that contain skips. Specifically, we're going to work with skips between the pitches Do, Mi and So

These exercises practice skips between Do, Mi and So, using syllable letters instead of notes. Sing each letter for one beat.

EXERCISE 43

EXERCISE 44

EXERCISE 45

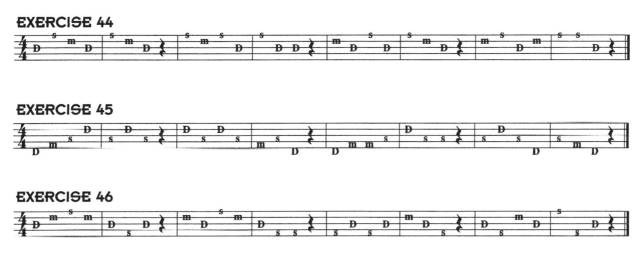

EXERCISE 46

EXERCISE 47

EXERCISE 48

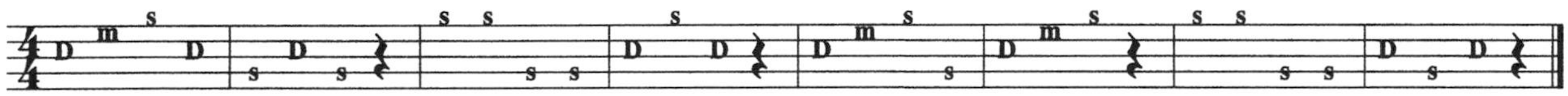

In reading Do-Mi-So skips with notes on the staff, it is very helpful to be aware of patterns in the line and space relationships of these notes. This and the term octave, are introduced below. Take a moment to study them.

STOP

The next three examples illustrate patterns in how Do, Mi, and So appear on the staff. An awareness of these line and space relationships aids reading these skips.

If Do is on a line then Mi is on the first line above Do, and So is on the second line above Do. Likewise, if Do is on a space, Mi is on the first space above Do, and So is on the second space above Do.

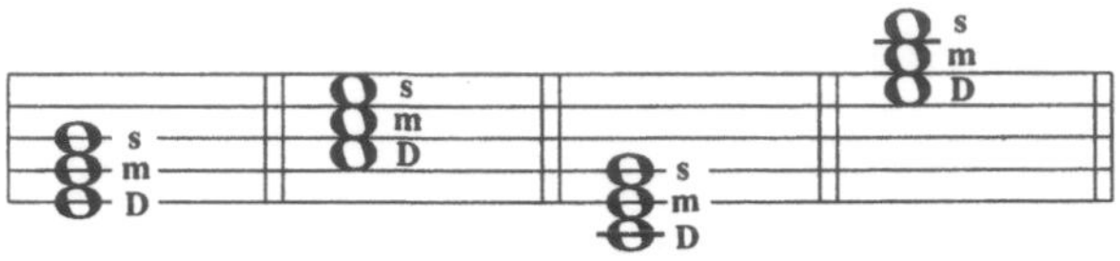

When we sing a scale, we start on a "low-pitched" Do and end on a "high pitched" Do. The distance between these two Do's is said to be an **octave**. The octave Do to Do and the octave So to So are two of the skips we'll be practicing. It's helpful in reading octave skips to be aware that one of the pitches is on a line and the other is on a space.

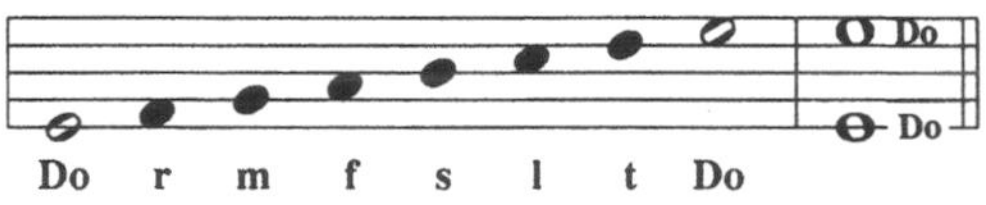

Examples of Octaves

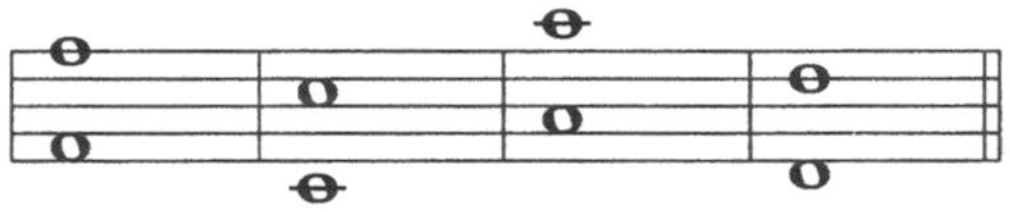

If Do is on a space, the So above it is also on a space, but the So below Do will be on a line. If Do is on a line, the So above it is also on a line, but the So below Do will be on a space.

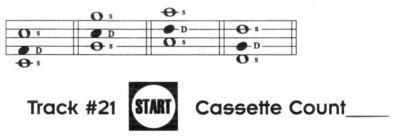

Track #21 START Cassette Count____

The next series of exercises practice skips between Do, Mi and So, using notes on the staff.

EXERCISE 49

EXERCISE 50

EXERCISE 51

EXERCISE 52

Thus far, you've been given the syllable name for the starting pitch of each exercise. You may have been wondering, "How do you know the name of the first pitch?" A musical symbol called the **key signature** can be used to identify it. See below for explanation.

STOP

The **key signature** is a cluster of **sharps** or **flats**. A key signature consists of up to seven sharps or flats, but not a combination of both. In music, the key signature is located at the beginning of a piece of music, just to the left of the meter signature.

The sharps or flats of a key signature are staggered from left to right on various lines and spaces of the staff. It is the last sharp or flat — the last one on the right — that will help us name the notes in the music.

a key signature of sharps: a key signature of flats.

The following examples show key signatures made up of sharps. *In a key signature of sharps, the last sharp is always on the line or space where **Ti** is located in that particular scale or key.* To name a note on any other line or space, simply move by step from the location of ti — naming the syllables as you go — until you have named the note you want to identify. Remember, when going *up* on the staff, name the scale tones in the order D r m f s l t D. When going *down* on the staff, say them in backwards order: D t l s f m r D.

Each of the examples below has three notes on the staff with the syllable name of each note identified. Study the examples of sharp key signatures to see how they were identified.

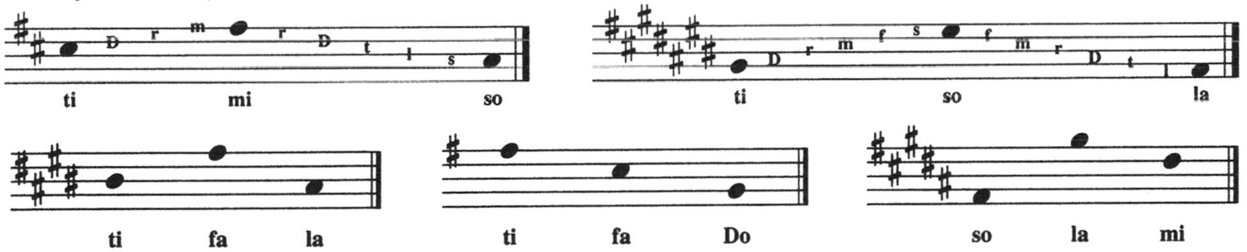

The following examples show key signatures made up of flats. *In a key signature of flats, the last flat is always on the line or space where **Fa** is located in that scale (**key**).* Otherwise the procedure for identifying notes is the same. Study the examples of flat key signatures to see how they were identified.

In the remainder of the exercises, the name of the starting pitch is no longer given. Stop the recording after each exercise and use the key signature in the next exercise to determine the name of its starting note. You'll find out in the recorded introduction to the exercise if you were correct.

Track #22 START Cassette Count____

Beginning with the next exercise, movement by step and skip is combined.

EXERCISE 53

The repeat sign with double dots that we've used so far has been at the end of an exercise, indicating a repeat from the beginning. Exercise 54 has a pair of repeat signs. A pair of repeat signs indicates a repeat of only the music between the two signs. In this exercise, sing from the beginning, straight to the second sign at the end. Then go back to the first sign and repeat the music between the two signs.

EXERCISE 54

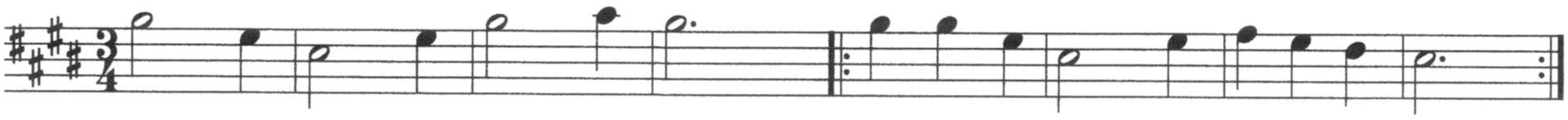

Exercise 55 introduces two new symbols which refer to styles of performance. In **staccato** singing or playing, the notes are performed in a short, detached manner. The symbol for staccato is a dot above or below the note head, opposite the stem.

Legato style is the opposite of staccato; the notes are sung in a sustained, smoothly-connected manner. Legato is the usual style of singing and does not normally require any special indication. However, there is a symbol that is sometimes used to indicate legato style. It is a curved line, called a **slur** and indicates that all notes within it are to be sung or played legato.

The slur looks the same as the tie, but their effect is different. The tie connects two notes of the same pitch, combining their note values as if they were a single note. A slur embraces two or more different pitches, indicating they should be performed legato.

EXERCISE 55

EXERCISE 56

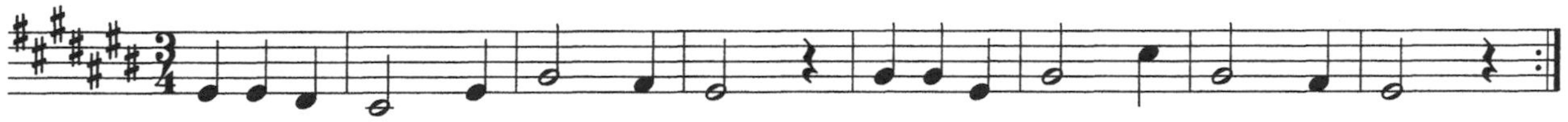

STOP

Exercise 57 uses a repeat sign with two endings. The measures that are bracketed (and numbered 1 and 2) are first and second endings. Here is how to read it:

1. Sing from the beginning to the end of the first ending.
2. At the repeat sign (at the end of the first ending), go back to the beginning for the repeat.
3. The second time through, skip over the first ending and sing the second ending.

Track #23 START Cassette Count____

EXERCISE 57

EXERCISE 58

STOP

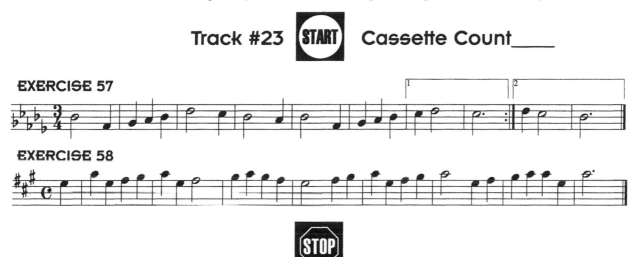

Up to this point, we have worked with what is called **relative pitch**. With relative pitch, Do can be any pitch we want it to be, BUT — once the pitch for Do is set, the other pitches of the scale (re, mi, fa, so, la, and ti) are automatically determined *in relation to where Do is.* Each of them is always the same distance from Do. Re is always a step above; La is two steps below, etc. They are each set *relative* to where Do is, hence the term relative pitch.

When we work with relative pitch — as we do with solfège — we name pitches with syllable names: Do, re, mi, fa, so, la, ti. Number names may also be used with relative pitch.

There is another way to consider pitch, and that is to say that every note on the staff represents a pitch that is very specific in its highness or lowness. Do, in a notated exercise, is not whatever pitch we want it to be. It is a very precise pitch. In fact, every notated pitch represents a pitch that can be played correctly by only one of the 88 keys on a piano.

This other way of looking at pitch is called **absolute pitch**. When we refer to the absolute pitch of notes, we name the notes with letters: A B C D E F and G (After G, start over with A). The letter name and the pitch can be modified with sharps ♯ and flats ♭. For example: F♯ is higher than F, B♭ is lower than B.

Symbols called **clefs** are used in notation to indicate the letter names of the staff lines and spaces. There are two that are commonly used: the **treble clef** and the **bass clef**. The clef sign appears at the beginning of the staff. The following example contains two staffs (or staves) with these clefs. The treble clef is on the first staff, and the bass clef is on the second staff. Pitches on the bass clef staff are lower than those on the treble clef staff. As was the case with low Do to high Do, the distance from any letter-named pitch to its next occurrence above or below is called an **octave**.

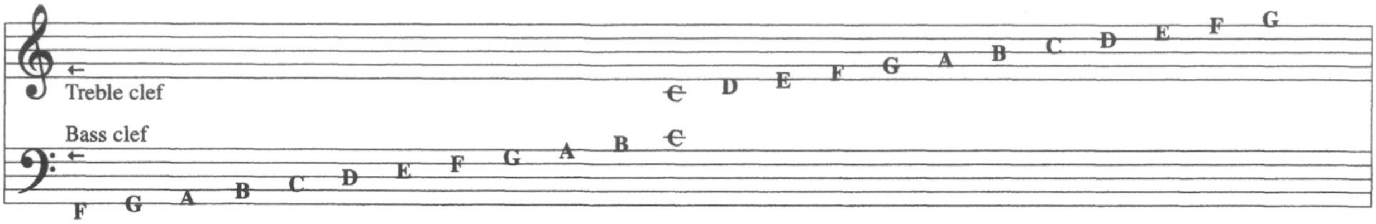

The point of this discussion of relative and absolute pitch is simply to make you aware that there are two sets of names we can apply to pitch. The letter names are the normal expression of pitch in music. The syllable names are used in the solfège method of reading music.

One final point about pitch: the use now of clefs in our exercises means that the notes represent precise pitches. But in order to give you practice reading notes all over the staff, and yet keep the pitches comfortable for your voice, the pitch level of the exercises may be adjusted from what is notated. To change the pitch of a piece of music to a higher or lower key (scale) is to **transpose** it.

Track #24 START Cassette Count____

EXERCISE 59

STOP

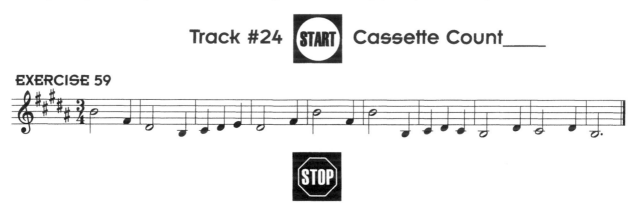

It was pointed out earlier that key signatures are made up of sharps or flats. There is a key signature, however, that has *no* sharps or flats. In this key signature, Do is on the line or space where the pitch C is located. *If you don't see any sharps or flats, Do is on the line or space where C is located.* Check the type of clef used on the staff, and then refer to the staff above to see where C is located on the staff. In Exercise 60, the first pitch is C and is therefore Do.

Track #25 START Cassette Count____

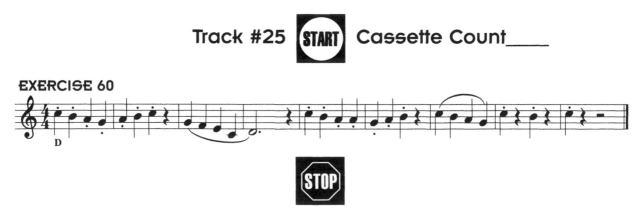

EXERCISE 60

STOP

Exercises 61 and 62 are bracketed together to show they can be sung as a duet. Learn each melody separately, then play one exercise while you sing the other. Then try it the other way around.

Track #26 START **Cassette Count____**

EXERCISE 61

EXERCISE 62

The next exercise uses eighth notes. See below to learn about them.

STOP

All of our exercises thus far have used the notes valued at 1, 2, 3 and 4 beats. Our last set of exercises include a new note value: the eighth note. Eighth notes are either connected with a *beam* or they have *flags*. The value of eighth notes is the same whether beamed or flagged.

Eighth Notes:

The duration of an eighth note is one-half beat. We will practice them in pairs. The combined duration of two eighth notes is the same as one quarter note. To put it another way, mathematically speaking, two eighths equal one fourth.

$$\frac{1}{8} + \frac{1}{8} = \frac{2}{8} = \frac{1}{4}$$

Our method for counting rhythms counts eighth notes in this way:

- The *first* eighth in a pair will be called by the number of the beat in the measure that it falls on.
- The second eighth in the pair is called "and."

Start the recording to count the rhythm of Exercises 63 and 64 before singing them.

Track #27 START Cassette Count____

Exercise 63, counted.

EXERCISE 63

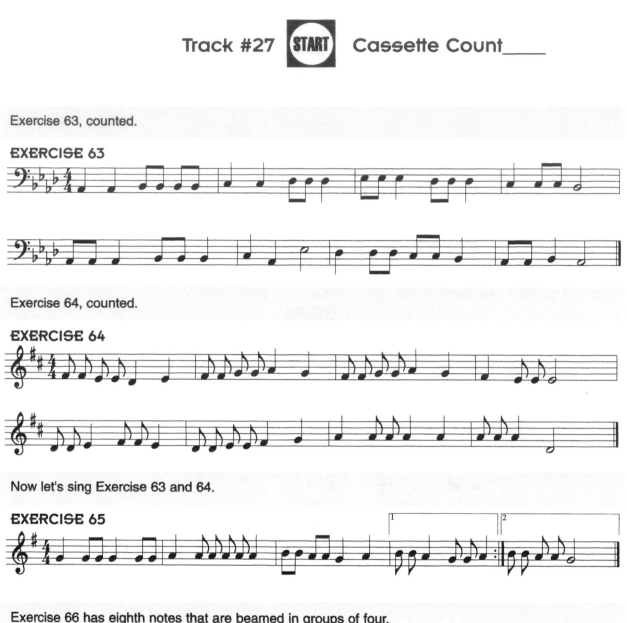

Exercise 64, counted.

EXERCISE 64

Now let's sing Exercise 63 and 64.

EXERCISE 65

Exercise 66 has eighth notes that are beamed in groups of four.

EXERCISE 66

STOP

Track #28 START Cassette Count____

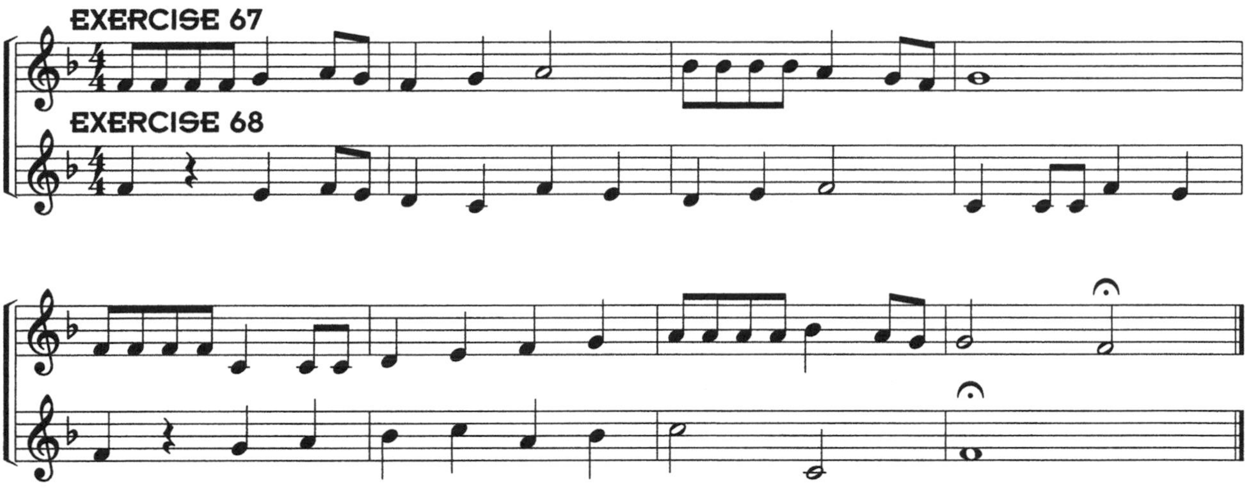

Exercises 67 and 68 can be sung as a duet.

This brings us to the end of *Sight Singing Made Simple*. We hope you've found this course beneficial, and we wish you the best in your musical endeavors.

STOP

NAME THAT TUNE!

The following four melodies are songs you probably know. Try sight singing each melody and see if you can name the song. First, try to sing the melody *mentally*; try to hear each pitch in your mind. Then try to sing it vocally with syllable names. Follow a similar procedure to the one used in the recorded exercises:

1. Sing Do and then Do-mi-so-mi-Do.
2. Sing the starting pitch.
3. Tap a moderately slow beat and begin sight singing the melody.

A pitch for Do in the lower part of your voice should work well for 1–3. For number 4, try pitching Do in the middle of your voice.

These melodies are not on the recording. The answers are on page 44.

GLOSSARY OF TERMS

absolute pitch – the specific highness or lowness of pitch, as measured by its rate of vibration. In music, absolute pitch is designated by letter names and accidentals: C G♯ E♭

accent – > stress or emphasize notes by singing or playing them louder.

accidentals – signs used to show the alteration of pitches; e.g., sharp ♯ raises pitch one half step, flat ♭ lowers pitch one half step, natural ♮ returns note to its normal pitch.

bar – see measure.

bar line – a vertical line placed on the staff to indicate the end of one measure and the beginning of another. A double bar (one thin and one thick) indicates the end of the music.

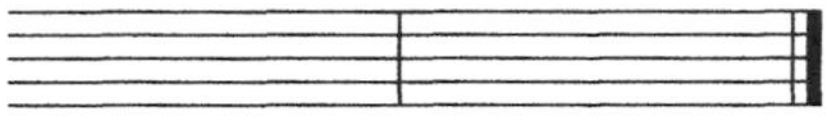

bass clef – 𝄢 see clef.

beat – the "pulse" of music to which a listener may clap or tap. It is the unit used to measure the time element in music. Note values, for example, are measured by the number of beats or portion of a beat they are worth.

chord – three or more pitches sounding simultaneously. For example, Do, Mi and So sounded together.

clef – a sign placed on a particular line of the staff to locate a specific (absolute) pitch. Other pitches are determined in relation to it. The two most common clefs are the **treble clef** and the **bass clef**.

common time – $\frac{4}{4}$ meter, indicated in the time signature with the symbol 𝄴

double bar – see bar line

duration – refers to the length of time a note value is held out. Duration is measured by the beat.

fermata – 𝄐 [fur-MAH-tah] hold the note (for longer than its value).

flat – ♭ see accidentals.

key – a set of pitches organized around a central pitch, called the keynote, that is characterized by stability and restfulness, e.g., Do. Key is similar in meaning to scale.

key signature – the group of sharps or flats to the right of the clef sign which indicates the scale pitches for that key. In a key signature of no sharps and flats, the key is C and C is Do.

keynote – the pitch which is the tonal center of a key or scale. The first tone of a scale. A key is named after the keynote; for example in the key of F, the keynote is F. In movable do solfège the keynote is Do.

ledger lines – short lines used to extend the lines and spaces of the staff.

legato – [lay-GAH-toh] tones sung smoothly connected. May be indicated by a **slur**.

measure – a group of beats (usually 2, 3, or 4), the first of which is accented. Also called a **bar**. In notation the notes of each measure are set apart by bar lines.

melody – a succession of single musical tones, usually organized in an interesting and attractive manner, having a definite beginning and end. *adj.,* **melodic.**

meter – the grouping of beats by accents. Each measured group is begun with an accent, and in notation is shown as a **measure**. The number of beats per measure is given by the top number of the meter (time) signature.

meter signature – a sign consisting of two numbers which indicates meter. The top number is the number of beats (or total beats worth of time) per measure. The bottom number represents the note that equals one beat. Also called the **time signature**.

movable Do – the method of using syllable names in sight singing, in which the keynote (in major) is always designated Do. For example, in the key of A, A is Do; in the key of E, E is Do.

notation – the graphic representation of music using notes and rests, as well as various other symbols including the staff, bar lines, clefs, meter and key signatures, and accidentals.

note & rest values – notes and rests are symbols used to represent duration of musical sounds and silence. The values of notes and rests are relative rather than absolute.

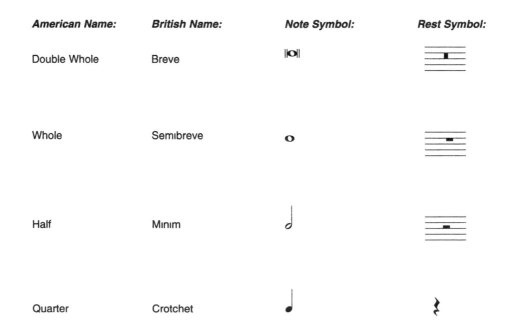

American Name:	***British Name:***	***Note Symbol:***	***Rest Symbol:***
Double Whole	Breve		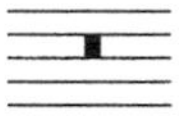
Whole	Semibreve		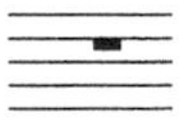
Half	Minim		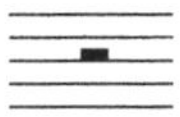
Quarter	Crotchet		

American Name:	*British Name:*	*Note Symbol:*	*Rest Symbol:*
Eighth	Quaver	𝅘𝅥𝅮	𝄾
Sixteenth	Semiquaver	𝅘𝅥𝅯	𝄿
Thirty-second	Demisemiquaver	𝅘𝅥𝅰	𝅀
Sixty-fourth	Hemidemisemiquaver	𝅘𝅥𝅱	𝅁

nomenclature of a note:

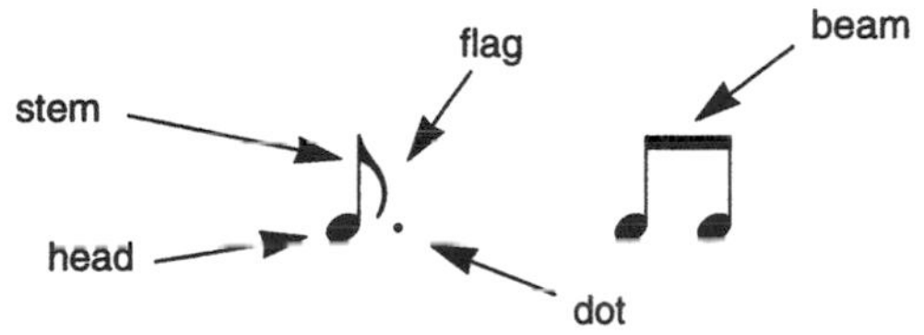

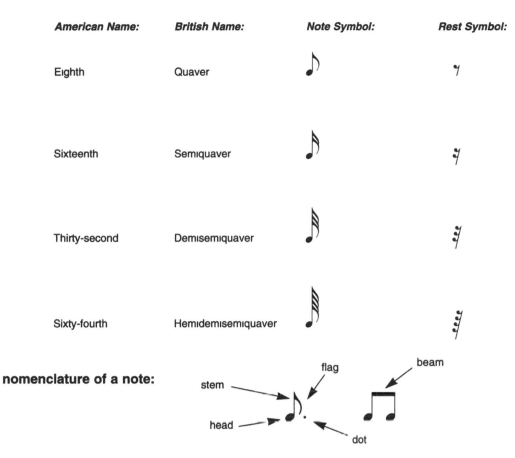

numbers – in solfège, numbers used instead of syllables are:

1 = Do   2 = re   3 = mi   4 = fa   5 = so   6 = la   7 = ti

octave – the distance between a pitch and the next occurrence of the pitch with the same name, seven steps away. For example, from a "low-pitched" Do to a "high-pitched" Do (seven steps above) is an octave.

pick-up – the last beat(s) in a measure.

pitch – the highness or lowness of musical sound, determined by the rate or frequency of vibration. In music, pitch is designated by letter names and accidentals (B♭, C, G♯). In solfège, pitches are sung with syllable names or numbers.

relative pitch – Do can be any pitch, all other pitches are determined in relation to where Do is.

repeat signs – repeat the section within the repeat marks. If the first one is omitted, repeat from the beginning.

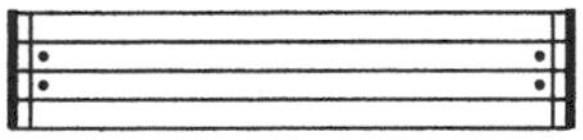

At the end of the first ending (bracket 1), repeat; on the repeat, skip the first ending; sing the second ending in its place.

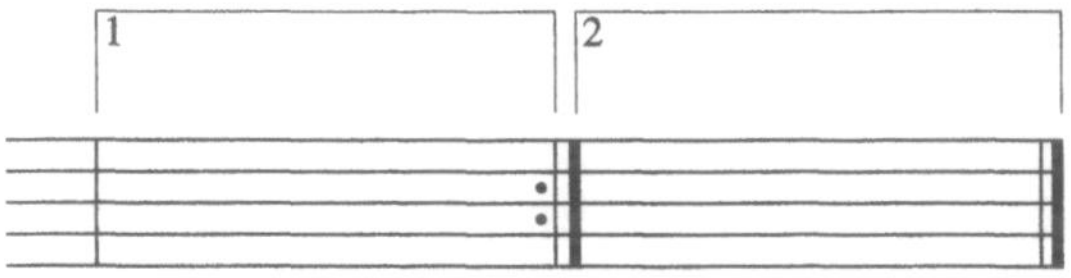

rest – see note and rest values.

rhythm – rhythm pertains to the time element in music. It covers (1) duration of the musical sounds, which is measured by the length or speed of the beat (tempo); and (2) meter, which is the result of accenting selected beats.

scale – a set of pitches used to compose a piece of music. An arrangement of pitches in a succession resulting in a specific pattern of steps. See **key**.

sharp – ♯ see accidentals.

sight reading – the ability to read (sing or play) music at "first sight," i.e., without prior preparation. *Sight singing* refers specifically to vocal sight reading.

sight singing – see sight reading.

slur – a curved line indicating that the notes within it are to be sung legato.

skip – melodic movement larger than a step; e.g., Do to mi (which "skips" over re), so to Do (which "skips" over la and ti).

solfège – Fr. [sol-FEZH] It. **solfeggio** [sol-FEJ-ee-oh]. The study of sight singing through the use of (sol-fa) syllables.

staccato – [stah-KAH-toh] detach, separate the notes from one another. Staccato mark:

staff – (*pl.* staffs or staves) the five horizontal, parallel lines on which notes are placed to show pitch. For the purpose of reference, the lines and spaces are numbered from the bottom up.

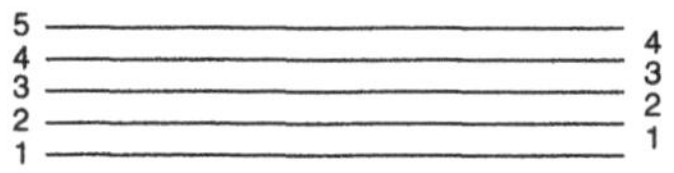

step – melodic movement to and from adjacent scale tones; e.g., Do *to* re, re *to* mi, ti *to* la, la *to* so, etc.

syllables – often called sol-fa syllables. Single syllable names given to the tones of a scale for use in sight singing training and practice. Syllables are notably used in solfège.

tempo – (*pl.* tempos or tempi) the speed at which a musical composition is performed. Tempo is determined by the duration of the beat.

tie – a curved line connecting two successive notes which are on the same line or space and are of identical pitch. Tied notes sound as if they were a single note of the combined value of the notes that are tied.

time signature – see meter signature.

tone – see pitch.

treble clef – 𝄞 see clef.

transpose – to rewrite or perform a composition in a key other than the original.

upbeat – see pick-up.

MISCELLANEOUS TERMS AND SYMBOLS

Sight Singing Made Simple has introduced two of the major elements of reading music: rhythm and pitch. A third and very important element is expression and interpretation. This includes dynamics (volume), tempo, phrasing, and timbre. Although it is not in the scope of this program to cover these aspects of music reading, a listing of the common terms and symbols that indicate them in notation is included here for reference.

I. Dynamics (volume)

pp (pianissimo) (pee-ah-NEE-see-moh) – very soft

p (piano) (pee-AH-no) – soft

mp (mezzo piano) (MEH-tsoh) – moderately soft

mf (mezzo forte) – moderately loud

f (forte) (FOR-teh) – loud

ff (fortissimo) (for-TEE-see-moh) – very loud

crescendo (cresc. ＜) (kreh-SHEN-doh) – get gradually louder

decrescendo (decresc. ＞) (day-kreh-SHEN-doh) – get gradually softer

diminuendo (dim.) (dee-mee-noo-EN-doh) – get gradually softer

morendo (moh-REN-doh) – dying away (in volume)

accent > stress by singing the note louder

marcato (mar-KAH-toh) – marked, accented

sforzando (sf sfz Λ) (sfor-TSAHN-doh) – a sudden, strong accent on a single note

II. Tempo (TEM-poh) refers to the speed of the beat. The first group of terms indicates the rate of the speed (in increasing order); the second group of terms indicates alterations of a steady tempo.

Very slow:	**Grave** (GRAH-veh)
	Largo (LAHR-goh)
Slow:	**Lento** (LEHN-toh)
	Adagio (ah-DAH-jee-oh)
Moderate:	**Andante** (ahn-Dahn-teh)
	Andantino (ahn-dahn-TEE-noh)
	Moderato (mah-deh-RAH-toh)
Moderately Fast:	**Allegretto** (ah-leh-GREH-toh)
Fast:	**Allegro** (ah-LAY-groh)
Very Fast:	**Vivace** (vee-VAH-cheh)
	Presto (PREH-stoh)
	Prestissimo (prehs-TEE-see-moh)

accelerando (accel.) (ah-cheh-leh-RAHN-doh) – gradually faster

allargando (allarg.) (ah-lahr-GAHN-doh) – growing slower, broader

rallentando (rall.) (rahl-en-TAHN-doh) – growing slower

ritardanto (rit. ritard.) (ree-tahr-DAHN-doh) – gradually slower

𝄐 **(fermata)** [fur-MAH-tah] – hold note (for longer than its value)

// – pause; a complete break

rubato (roo-BAH-toh) – freely; irregular movement of the beat

a tempo (ah TEM-poh) – return to the original tempo

III. Other Terms And Symbols

assai (ah-SAH-ee) – very

con (kohn) – with

divisi (div.) (dee-VEE-zee) – divide, the part divides

dolce (DOHL-cheh) – sweetly and softly

legato (lay-GAH-toh) – smoothly connected; may be indicated by a slur

maestoso (mah-ehs-STOH-soh) – majestic

meno (MAY-noh) – less

meno mosso (MAY-noh MAW-soh) – less speed

molto (MOHL-toh) – much, very

non (nohn) – not

piu (pew) – more

poco (POH-koh) – little

sempre (SEHM-preh) – always

simile (SEE-mee-leh) – like; in the same way

sostenuto (sohs-teh-NOO-toh) – sustained

staccato (stah-KAH-toh) – detached

subito (SOO-bee-toh) – suddenly

tenuto (teh-NOO-toh) – sustained; hold note(s) for the full value

troppo (TROH-poh) – too much

unison (unis.) – sing the same pitches (at the same time)

' – take a breath

n.b. (no breath) and ⌒ (dotted slur) – do not breathe here

NAME THAT TUNE! ANSWERS

1. Mary Had A Little Lamb
2. Twinkle, Twinkle Little Star
3. Jingle Bells
4. Brother John

ABOUT THE AUTHOR

David Bauguess

David Bauguess *(pronounced BAW-gus)* has been a choral director and an enthusiastic teacher of sight singing for over twenty-five years. Most of his teaching career has been at the secondary level in the Montrose County School District in Montrose, Colorado. He is the author of the best-selling *The Jenson Sight Singing Course,* also published by Hal Leonard, and he was a contributor to books 7 and 8 of *Music and You,* published by Macmillan. He is a member of the Voice Care Network and has been an active member and officer of the Colorado affiliates of the American Choral Directors Association and the Music Educators National Conference. He has presented sight singing clinics for many educational institutions and professional music organizations.

The author is grateful to Janet Klevberg and Emily Crocker at Hal Leonard Corporation for their support and assistance with the development and production of *Sight Singing Made Simple.*

Also by David Bauguess

THE JENSON SIGHT SINGING COURSE

Here's what they're saying about...

THE JENSON SIGHT SINGING COURSE

"Of the many sight singing courses which have been published in the past several years, I find none as effective as **THE JENSON SIGHT SINGING COURSE** by David Bauguess."

-Dr. C.M. Shearer
Choral Director, Kent State University

"David Bauguess has put forth an excellent case for teaching sight singing as a basis on which to build a better choral ensemble. The materials that he presents are fundamental, yet thorough enough for the choral educator to do just that."

-The Choral Journal

"**THE JENSON SIGHT SINGING COURSE** by David Bauguess is an excellent book! It is a classroom-tested and proven method for improving a choir's music reading abilities and overall musicianship."

-Robert L. Garretson
Author, Conducting Choral Music, 6th Ed.

This comprehensive method based on the solfége system (with optional numbers) gives you a step-by-step plan for teaching the fundamentals of sight singing.

Recommended for Grade 9-adult

47819012	Student Edition, Vol. I
47819029	Teacher's Edition, Vol. I

47819062	Student Edition, Vol. II
47819079	Teacher's Edition, Vol. II
47819104	Sight Singing Part Exercises